Virtual Reality Quantum Physics

Unveiling the Mysteries of the Universe

Table of Contents

Chapter 1. Introduction

Dive into the uncharted territories of the cosmos through our Special Report: "Virtual Reality Quantum Physics: Unveiling the Mysteries of the Universe". This edifying exploration captures the intersection of cutting-edge technology and sophisticated yet confounding science - making it a seminal guide for those enthralled by the vast wonders of the universe. Fear no technical jargon, as we've stripped down complex quantum mechanics to accessible, everyday language, bringing the exhilarating world of subatomic particles to your fingertips. Prepare to traverse the quantum realm like never before, visiting those convoluted corners that confound even prominent scientists. Don't miss this unique opportunity to explore the unfathomable - made conceivable by virtual reality. So, are you ready to unravel the fabric of reality? This special report awaits you.

Chapter 2. From Newton to Quantum: A Historical Overview

To appreciate the road from Newtonian Physics to Quantum Physics, we must go on a journey that begins as early as the 17th century, which arguably marks the birth of modern science. Quench your thirst of knowledge as we delve into significant names, ideas, and transformative epochs that carved the path to our comprehension of quantum physics today.

2.1. Classical Physics: Newton's Legacy

Renowned English scientist Sir Isaac Newton, born in 1642, shook the pillars of understanding during his lifetime with his revolutionary contribution to physics. The universe, according to Newton, operated like a majestic clock, wound up by God and ever ticking via immutable laws.

His 'Principia Mathematica' published in 1687, formalized three laws of motion that set the foundation for the study of mechanics. His universal law of gravitation became the blueprint for understanding celestial bodies' motions - a significant leap in the field of astronomy. Newton's deterministic model ruled until the close of the 19th century, during which another prodigy posited an upheaval of the scientific community.

2.2. A Crack in the Paradigm: The Advent of Electromagnetism

In 1865, James Clerk Maxwell put forth a unified theory of electromagnetism, shattering the Newtonian model's comfort. Maxwell's equations described how magnetic and electric fields interact, giving us a new lens to look at light. Light was an electromagnetic wave, traveling at a consistent speed regardless of the observer's movement. Maxwell's work opened Pandora's box, inviting the development of modern technologies like radio, television, and radar.

2.3. Enter Planck: The Quantum Riddle Begins

The turn of the 20th century saw an unexpected twist in the tale with Max Planck's hitherto unfamiliar concept - the quantum. An anomaly known as the ultraviolet catastrophe troubling the realm of black body radiation brought Planck to propose this radical concept. Planck suggested energy was not continuous but discrete, divisible into elemental "quanta."

Planck's revolutionary proposal inadvertently birthed a new theory. The notion of energy quanta implied that the universe was not the smooth fabric Newton depicted but more like a choppy sea, woven from tiny, discrete threads of energy.

2.4. Albert Einstein and the Photoelectric Effect

Albert Einstein, the iconic physicist who would later become synonymous with genius, built upon Planck's quantum idea. In 1905, Einstein addressed the photoelectric effect phenomenon - an area where classical theory faltered. He proposed that light wasn't just a wave but also a particle (photon) carrying specific energy quanta, depending on its frequency.

This dual nature of light, as both particle and wave, set the stage for the transition into quantum physics. This concept, called wave-particle duality, was shocking, yet it fit experimental evidence that classical theories could not explain.

2.5. Niels Bohr and the Quantum Atom

The Danish physicist Niels Bohr, equipped with the quantum concept, challenged the conventional atomic model. According to classical physics, an electron in an atom should radiate away its energy, spiral into the nucleus, and collapse the atom - an absurdity against nature's law. Bohr stepped beyond the classical frame, declaring that electrons in atoms occupy specific energy levels, or shells, without intermediate states.

2.6. The Age of Uncertainty: Heisenberg's Principle

Heisenberg's uncertainty principle in the 1920s further widened the gap between classical and quantum physics. According to him, there's a fundamental limit to how accurately we can know a particle's position and momentum simultaneously. Contradicting the determinism of Newtonian physics, Heisenberg's quantum realm appeared wrapped in probabilities and uncertainties.

2.7. A Paradigm Shift: Enter Quantum Mechanics

The 1920s marked a turning point as scientists began to abandon attempts to shove quantum phenomena into the classical box. Quantum mechanics fully bloomed, celebrating the oddity of waves acting as particles and particles infiltrating waves.

Quantum mechanics carved a universe where particles could be in multiple places at the same time (superposition), where particles could instantly affect each other's state regardless of distance (entanglement), and where reality existed only as a haze of probability until observed. The theory was downright bizarre but predictively powerful. It has passed multiple tests and made possible innovations such as lasers and semiconductors that form the backbone of modern tech and communication.

Our journey has brought us from Newton's predictably clockwork universe to the perplexing quantum realm where the fantastic is ordinary. Although we have only scratched the surface of this captivating tale, it suffices to highlight the leaps of paradigm shifts our understanding of the universe has undergone. The tale of physics, from Newton to Quantum, is full of mind-stretching concepts, monumental discoveries, and an overwhelming realization of how much more there is to decipher in our mesmerizing cosmos.

Chapter 3. Entering the Quantum Realm: Basics of Quantum Physics

Our entry into the captivating domain of quantum physics commences by introducing some primary, yet powerful, principles. These crux doctrines weave the complex tapestry of this seemingly inscrutable discipline.

3.1. The Dual Nature of Matter and Light

The concept of wave-particle duality is one of the fascinating characteristics of quantum mechanics. A wave-like nature embodies all particles exhibiting properties of both particles and waves. The prime example is light itself, traditionally considered purely a wave but found to act like a particle in certain situations. Conversely, solid particles, considered the epitome of material, such as electrons, can also display wave-like properties. This predilection for particles to exhibit both particle and wave-like characteristics forms the bedrock of quantum physics.

3.2. Quantum Superposition

In classical physics, objects exist in determinate states—a ball, for instance, is at a chosen location at a specific given time. However, in the quantum realm, particles can be in several positions simultaneously, a bizarre phenomenon known as quantum superposition. The superposition collapses into a definitive state only when observed or measured, a fact accentuated by the famous mental experiment 'Schrodinger's Cat Experiment.'

3.3. Quantum Entanglement

Entanglement might seem like a plot straight out of a science fiction novel but is an integral part of quantum physics. Put simply, two (or more) particles can become entangled, sharing a bond so intricate that they instantaneously affect each other, no matter the distance separating them. Albert Einstein termed this 'spooky action at a distance.' Despite sounding spooky, entanglement could be a mighty tool for developing powerful quantum computers or building secure communication networks.

3.4. Schrödinger's Equation

Schrödinger's Equation is the mathematical tool that explores and explains these phenomena. It provides a way to calculate the wave function of a system and how it changes over time, a pivotal accomplishment in quantifying the inherently fuzzy quantum world.

3.5. The Uncertainty Principle

Werner Heisenberg's uncertainty principle is another quintessential component of quantum theory. It highlights the impossibility of precisely measuring simultaneously both the momentum and position of a particle. The more accurately we know one of these values, the less accurately we know the other.

3.6. Quantum Fields and Quantum Field Theory

Underneath it all are quantum fields. Every particle in the universe has a corresponding field, and particles themselves can be seen as excitations of those corresponding fields. Quantum Field Theory (QFT) is the language used to describe these dynamics.

3.7. Quantum Teleportation: Science Fact or Fiction?

One of the most tantalizing concepts within the quantum realm is quantum teleportation. Though it isn't anything like what you've seen in the movies, the quantum version involves transferring quantum information from one location to another – without traversing the physical space between.

3.8. Harnessing the Quantum Realm: Tools and Technology

While it's traditionally been tough to experiment and verify quantum theories due to the minuscule size and inherent weirdness of the quantum world, technology is catching up. Quantum tunneling microscopes, particle accelerators, and quantum computers are among the tools scientists use to illuminate the mysteries of the quantum world today.

3.9. Uncloaking the Quantum Mysteries: The Future of Quantum Physics

At present, we still don't comprehend everything about the quantum realm. Questions about quantum gravity and how to successfully integrate quantum mechanics with Einstein's General Theory of Relativity are among the unanswered queries. Researchers also grapple with the interpretations of quantum mechanics, which can be, in many instances, debatable. Future theoretical and experimental pursuits will hopefully provide answers and continue to expand our understanding eliminating ambiguities.

In conclusion, quantum physics is a peculiar, confounding, yet endlessly fascinating field, presenting us with a description of physical reality that defies common sense and what we're accustomed to. It finds applications in modern technologies and promises to revolutionize the future in ways unimagined. However, the technical language and mathematical complexity often discourages people from delving into this fascinating realm. Through this report, we have tried to demystify the mysteries of the quantum landscape while sowing seeds of curiosity in you to kindle further exploration. Each section here can be elaborated into whole books, and the story of quantum discovering itself is unwinding in labs and institutions across the globe as you read this.

Here ends the journey into the fundamentals of quantum physics. However, the quest for knowledge should not rest. Treading onward, we'd be exploring the practical applications of quantum mechanics in our everyday lives and the transformative potential it offers in the chapters to come.

Chapter 4. Virtual Reality: Audacious Enabler of Immersive Technologies

Virtual reality (VR) represents an audacious leap forward in our ability to experience and interact with digital constructs. As a groundbreaking technological medium, it empowers humans to embark on sensory journeys that spatially and visually transcend the limits of the physical world. VR's immersive qualities allow us to explore realms from the comfort of our homes, making it an ideal enabler of our quest to understand, experience, and share the complex and captivating world of quantum physics.

4.1. The Evolution of Virtual Reality

The birth of virtual reality dates back to the mid-20th century, with Morton Heilig's Sensorama - a large, arcade-style machine offering multisensory experiences. However, the technology only really gained attraction in the late 1980s when Jaron Lanier's VPL Research started selling VR goggles and gloves. This marked the inception of virtual reality as we know it today.

The technology then saw considerable advancements during the 2010s, fueled by rapidly evolving computer technology and digital graphics. Devices like the Oculus Rift, HTC Vive, and PlayStation VR brought high-quality VR experiences directly to consumers. Nevertheless, VR's potential extends far beyond gaming and entertainment - to realms as diverse and complex as architecture, rehabilitation, and indeed, the enigmatic domain of quantum physics.

4.2. Understanding Virtual Reality

In essence, virtual reality furnishes users with simulated experiences that can be similar to or entirely different from the real world. Devices such as VR headsets are typically used for this purpose, offering stereoscopic displays that create an immersive 3D environment. Advanced headsets also provide surround sound, haptic feedback, and motion tracking to enhance the sense of reality.

It's important to differentiate VR from augmented reality (AR) and mixed reality (MR). AR overlays digital information onto the real world, while MR blends real and virtual worlds to produce new environments where physical and digital objects coexist and interact. VR, however, completely substitutes the user's environment with a simulated one.

4.3. The Technology Behind the Scene

Virtual reality relies primarily on two fundamental technologies: tracking and rendering.

Tracking refers to the process of detecting a user's movements and translating them into the virtual environment. Techniques like infrared tracking, accelerometers, and gyroscopes are used for this purpose. Advanced VR systems also incorporate motion sensing and eye tracking to produce highly responsive and user-friendly experiences.

Rendering, on the other hand, involves producing the graphics that the user sees in the VR headset. Modern VR systems lean heavily on computer power to generate high-resolution, lifelike images at high frame rates. This fusion of speed and detail creates a convincing illusion of reality, making VR systems particularly suitable for simulating quantum physics experiments.

4.4. Virtual Reality & Quantum Physics: A Promising Union

The complexity of quantum mechanics often proves bewildering even for scientists who have dedicated their lives to its study. Concepts such as superposition and quantum entanglement are notoriously difficult to visualize and comprehend. This is where VR can step in and offer a uniquely immersive perspective.

Imagine observing the quantum superposition – the notion that a particle can exist in two places at once before it's measured. Conventional teaching often leaves students stumped due to the lack of experimental evidence. However, using VR technology enables them to step into a hyper-realistic quantum world, observe these phenomena firsthand, and truly grasp their utterly counterintuitive nature.

Similarly, VR can open a gateway to better comprehend quantum entanglement. This principle, which Einstein famously dubbed "spooky action at a distance," seems to link particles across even the vastest expanses, instantaneously. A well-crafted VR simulation can demonstrate this effect and better contextualize both its importance and its baffling aspects.

Indeed, virtual reality's capacity to simulate and visualize intricate quantum behaviors presents a potent tool for exploring, teaching, and perhaps pushing the boundaries of this crucially significant and yet perplexing sector of physics.

In conclusion, VR stands as a ground-breaking technology poised to change how we engage with the complex theories of quantum physics. By leveraging its profound capacity to immerse users wholly into a meticulously created digital environment, VR offers us a new, promising route to decipher quantum physics' enigmatic mysteries. Its potential to pivot quantum physics education and research marks the beginning of a thrilling epoch, where technology and science interweave to generate deeper insights into the fabric of reality.

Chapter 5. Merging Worlds: The Intersection of Quantum Physics and Virtual Reality

The continuous evolution of technology is enabling us to view and comprehend our reality in a completely new way. This convergence brings two significant areas of study into focus: quantum physics, the study of the universe at its most elementary level, and virtual reality (VR), a technology that cloaks our senses and transports us into an artificial world.

5.1. Quantum Physics: An Overview

Quantum physics, also known as quantum mechanics, dives deep into the research of particles at the quantum level - particles smaller than atoms. It introduced the concept of wave-particle duality, which suggests that all particles exhibit both particle and wave characteristics. It further speaks about superposition, where a quantum particle exists in multiple states at the same time until observed. Quantum entanglement, another strange phenomenon, states that entangled particles can affect each other's states instantaneously, regardless of the distance separating them. These fascinating yet baffling concepts shifted the paradigm of previously established Newtonian physics, seeking explanations for the smaller particles in the universe.

5.2. Virtual Reality: Immersive Technology

On the other hand, virtual reality replaces our world with a simulated one. It provides a sense of immersion that allows users to interact with 3D world objects using VR gear such as headsets and gloves. The science behind VR is about tricking the human senses into perceiving digital content as real by replicating sight, sound, touch, and sometimes even smell. Applications of VR extend across numerous industries - from education and healthcare to entertainment and tourism, and many more.

5.3. Bridging the Two Worlds

The intersection of quantum physics and virtual reality is an exciting frontier that has the potential to revolutionize the way we perceive and interact with the quantum world. Scientists and researchers are exploring this amalgamation in several ways.

5.3.1. Visualizing Quantum Phenomena

Quantum mechanics is notorious for its intricacy and conceptual abstractions. Its fundamental entities, quantum particles, cannot be observed by the naked eye. Here's where VR can play a pivotal role in enabling us to visualize these complex phenomena. By translating quantum data into an immersive 3D world, we can construct realistic models of quantum particles and their peculiar behavior. For learners, this could mean a more intuitive understanding of quantum conundrums, which were previously impossible or extremely complicated to visualize.

5.4. Quantum Computing and VR

One of the major implications of quantum mechanics in technology is the development of quantum computers. These machines leverage the principles of superposition and entanglement to process vast amounts of data simultaneously, exponentially faster than conventional computers. However, understanding and programming quantum computers is a complex task. This is where VR can prove instrumental. By utilizing VR to simulate a quantum computer's operation, developers can gain a more profound understanding of quantum algorithms. They can oversee the processing and computation in a virtually created space, making quantum computing more accessible.

5.5. Simulating Quantum Experiments

Scientists presently rely on complex and expensive experimental setups to observe and affirm theoretical constructs of quantum mechanics. However, setting up these experiments can be tedious and time-consuming. Additionally, some experiments can be limited by constraints in technology and development. Here, VR can be a game-changer. Scientists could perform simulations of these experiments in a virtual quantum lab. Such simulated experiments will lower costs and time needed, accelerating the development and understanding of quantum mechanics.

5.6. Enhancing Quantum Intuition

A significant impediment faced by quantum physics students and researchers alike is developing intuition about quantum phenomena. Since these phenomena do not have a direct analogue in our day-to-day experiences, it becomes difficult to form an intuitive understanding. Virtual reality, with its immersive nature, can create environments that can help users develop this intuition. Visually flying through a 3D quantum system or manipulating quantum states and variables in a virtual lab could lead to profound insights and breakthroughs. Not to mention how it makes the learning and research experience a lot more exciting!

5.7. The Quantum VR Revolution

The explorations into the merger of quantum physics and virtual reality are nascent yet promising. New quantum VR simulations are being designed and launched, such as the Quantum Chess game that incorporates quantum superposition and entanglement - previously abstract concepts - into its gameplay. The Quantum VR project at Google aims to create VR software that would allow users to experience what it is like inside a quantum computer, manipulating qubits in a 3D environment.

Despite the exciting benefits and potential outcomes of the union between quantum physics and virtual reality, this interdisciplinary field is still in its infanthood, and there are challenges to overcome. Reliable and scalable quantum hardware is still being developed, as is VR technology which can fully simulate quantum processes. However, the future of this merger shines brightly, with the potential to revolutionize education, research, computing, and perhaps even unsettle our understanding of reality itself.

As quantum physicist Niels Bohr once mused, "If quantum mechanics hasn't profoundly shocked you, you haven't understood it yet." Perhaps with the coming age of Quantum VR, we might finally grasp and, in some sense, experience the shock that Bohr referenced all those years ago - this time, within a marvelous, simulated reality.

Chapter 6. Simulating Subatomic Adventure: Quantum Visualizations in VR

For centuries, scientists and thinkers have pondered over the enigmatic subatomic world. Quantum mechanics, a field of physics that deals with phenomena on a minuscule scale, has remained mystifying even to seasoned scientists. However, embracing cutting-edge technologies like Virtual Reality (VR) has opened new avenues to simulate and visually represent the otherwise baffling quantum phenomena – breaking down the elusive world of quantum physics into visually compelling and comprehensible experiences. Let's plunge into this subatomic adventure.

6.1. The Quantum World: An Overview

In the context of quantum physics, we deal with infinitesimal particles that exist in the fabric of the universe. These particles, including but not limited to electrons, photons, and quarks, follow an entirely different set of rules compared to what we observe in the macro world. Concepts such as superposition, wave-particle duality, and quantum entanglement – that exist only in the realm of the quantum – seemingly defy our everyday logical understanding of the physical world. These peculiar aspects can be scarcely grasped in a conventional learning context, creating a persistent barrier to mastering quantum mechanics.

However, the advent of VR technology has the potential to simplify these complexities by providing a more intuitive understanding of quantum behavior. VR can whisk us away to the heart of the quantum world, where we can interact with and visualize the behavior of these microcosmic entities.

6.2. VR Visualization of Quantum Phenomena

Virtual reality, being an immersive, multi-sensory experience, allows us to see and interact with quantum phenomena. Several VR experiences and simulations have been designed to represent different quantum phenomena:

- Superposition: Quantum superposition is a fundamental principle which suggests that any two (or more) quantum states can be added (superposed) to make another valid quantum state; and conversely, that every quantum state can be represented as a sum of two or more other distinct states. A VR experience can exhibit superposition by having the user observe a particle existing in multiple places simultaneously.

- Quantum Entanglement: One of the most bizarre features of the quantum world is entanglement, where two particles become inextricable, and the state of one instantaneously influences the state of the other, no matter the distance between them. Entanglement in a VR environment could be demonstrated by manipulating one particle and having the user observe the instant changes in the entangled partner.

- Wave-Particle Duality: Particles like photons and electrons exhibit both wave and particle characteristics. They can exist as particles at certain times and as waves at others. In a VR setup, one can visualize this dual nature by switching between views to observe the particle and wave states.

6.3. Quantum Uncertainty and Its VR Rendering

A peculiar and confounding phenomenon at the heart of quantum mechanics is the Heisenberg Uncertainty Principle. It highlights the fundamental limit on the precision with which certain pairs of physical properties, such as position and momentum, can be simultaneously known. In the quantum world, the act of measuring can disrupt these properties, making it impossible to precisely measure both at the same time.

VR can provide an exciting solution to this complex principle. By adopting quantized solutions and probabilistic distributions, VR simulations can represent the "cloud of probabilities" that embodies the uncertainty principle. Users can interact with a particle in these simulations, visually experiencing the state transformations of the particle as they attempt to measure its properties, vividly illustrating the essence of quantum uncertainty.

6.4. Application of Quantum Visualizations

The implementation of VR in demystifying quantum phenomena has several potential applications:

- Education: In a classroom setting, quantum VR experiences can supplement traditional teaching methods to provide an intuitive understanding of quantum principles.

- Research: Researchers can use VR to visually model quantum systems and perform simulations that might lead to breakthroughs in quantum science.

- Public Outreach: For persons interested in science, VR quantum visualizations can serve as edutainment, quenching their thirst for absorbing scientific knowledge.

6.5. Conclusion: Unveiling the Quantum Realm

As we edge closer to fully understanding the quantum world, Virtual Reality has proven to be an essential tool for visualizing and intuitively comprehending challenging quantum phenomena. It brings science to the tips of our fingers, making the peculiarities of quantum mechanics as accessible and understandable as the physics of our macro world.

Thus, the exploration of the quantum realm via Virtual Reality signifies an exciting frontier in both technological and quantum scientific advancements, translating abstract quantum principles into direct immersive experiences. This offers an unmatched educational tool, a sophisticated research instrument, and a fresh means of communication for public science engagement. The veil over the quantum world is gradually lifting – one VR simulation at a time.

Chapter 7. Decoding Quantum Mechanics: Making Sense of Schrodinger's Cat

Quantum mechanics, an intricate and perplexing facet of modern physics, often boggles the mind with its paradoxes and counterintuitive phenomena. Unquestionably, one of the most bewildering concepts under its spectrum is the paradox of Schrodinger's cat. This theoretical experiment, proposed by Nobel laureate Erwin Schrödinger, captures the gist of quantum superposition and entanglement - two challenging yet fundamental principles of quantum theory. So, saddle up for a thrilling journey as we scout through the labyrinth of Schrödinger's cat.

7.1. Understanding Quantum Superposition

At the core of Schrödinger's conception is quantum superposition, a principle that grants particles the ability to exist in multiple states simultaneously.

Particle State	Probability	Description
Upright	50%	The particle is in an upright position
Upside Down	50%	The particle is upside down
Both	100 %	The particle is both upright and upside down simultaneously

This is not your typical physical behavior observable in our daily lives but a characteristically quantum world's trait. This quirkiness aggrandizes when the particle doesn't manifest a definite state until measured - a peculiar act of observation solidifying reality.

7.2. The Experiment: A Cat, a Flask, and a Pin

Schrödinger's thought experiment revolves around a cat inside a sealed box alongside a radioactive source, a flask of poison, and a Geiger counter. The radioactive source has an equal probability of decaying or not.

In case it decays, it would trigger the Geiger counter, which would subsequently trigger the release of poison, killing the cat. Conversely, if the radioactive source doesn't decay, the sequence doesn't proceed, leaving the cat alive.

7.3. Quantum Superposition: The Dead and "Alive" Cat

From a quantum viewpoint, the cat is both alive and dead until the box is opened - an instance of quantum superposition. This stems from the entanglement of the cat's state with the radioactive source.

7.4. Decoherence: Collapsing the Superposition

Reality, as we experience it, doesn't allow for a cat to be concurrently dead and alive. When observed, the superposition inexplicably collapses, rendering the cat either alive or dead.

This process of 'decoherence' demonstrates how quantum systems interact with their environment, forcing the system to conform to one state. Yet, before the observation, the cat is in a blurry blend of possibilities.

7.5. Quantum Entanglement: Intertwining of Fates

Not only does this paradox underscore superposition, but it also reveals another peculiar quantum behavior - quantum entanglement. Through this, quantum particles become inextricably linked, mirroring each other's states instantaneously, regardless of their distance.

7.6. Controversies and Interpretations

Such paradoxes and the quantum mechanics foundations led to several philosophical debates and interpretations regarding reality's nature. These interpretations range from Copenhagen interpretation, advocating a subjective view of quantum reality, to many-worlds interpretation, postulating the existence of infinite parallel universes.

Let's delve into the two primary interpretations:

7.6.1. Copenhagen Interpretation

The Copenhagen interpretation, adhered to by many quantum physicists, holds that it is the act of observation that collapses the wave function. Thus, the cat remains both dead and alive until someone peeks inside the box.

7.6.2. Many-Worlds Interpretation

Another alternative, the many-worlds interpretation, poses that for every quantum event, the universe splits to accommodate all possible outcomes. So, when the box is opened, the universe bifurcates into one where the cat is alive and another where it's not.

7.7. Impacts and Applications of Quantum Mechanics

Real-life applications of quantum mechanics are prevalent in our daily lives, even if their quantum nature is not always discernible. Quantum superposition forms the basis for quantum computing, which holds potential for enormous computational power. Quantum entanglement, on the other hand, can revolutionize communication technologies by carrying out unhackable quantum cryptography.

Despite the complexities and paradoxes, quantum mechanics provides us with a useful model for discerning the universe's most minute constituents. From Schrödinger's cat, we ascertain that quantum mechanics is not deterministic but riddled with probabilities. And that's what makes it an intriguing and complex domain, forever prodding our understanding of reality. It is within this inscrutability and profound nature that the allure of quantum physics lies, continually unfolding the universe's mysteries, one quantum at a time.

Chapter 8. Quantum Entanglement and Teleportation: A VR Experience

Diving straight into the world of quantum entanglement and teleportation, let's understand how these complex phenomena manifest in the quantum world. Remember, you're about to enter a realm where the conventional rules of physics cease to exist in their usual capacity, making room for mind-bending possibilities.

8.1. The Enigma of Quantum Entanglement

Quantum entanglement is a strange phenomenon that defies common sense and even Einstein's local realism, leading him to famously describe it as "spooky action at a distance". It involves a connection between particles such that the state of one instantaneously influences the state of the other, no matter how far apart they are.

To better comprehend this, let's visualize two entangled particles. You're in a VR space station floating between these two spheres of energy, representing the particles. Both spheres pulse in sync, changing colours together. This is a representation of their entangled state. If you observe the state of one (say, the colour), you immediately know the state of the other. In the quantum world, this happens regardless of the distance separating them.

8.2. Teleporting Quantum Information

Transitioning from entanglement, let's venture into quantum teleportation. Unlike the popular science fiction trope, quantum teleportation doesn't involve the transfer of matter. Rather, it's the transmission of information about a particle's state from one location to another.

In our VR simulation, imagine an avatar standing on the left end of the space station holding a square particle. Another avatar awaits on the opposite end. The first avatar will "teleport" the information about the particle to the second avatar, with the vital assistance of an entangled pair of particles.

In the center of the station, two entangled spheres pop into existence. Each avatar receives one sphere. The first avatar then performs a special operation, bringing the original square particle and its sphere together. This combined state is then 'measured', which affects the two spheres due to their entanglement.

A representation of this quantum measurement - the changing patterns of colours on the first avatar's sphere - is communicated to the second avatar. The second avatar then conducts specific operations on its sphere based on the received patterns, and voila! The square particle appears at the second avatar's location. The original square particle vanishes, demonstrating quantum no-cloning theorem: a theorem that states it's impossible to create an identical copy of any unknown quantum state.

8.3. Interpreting Quantum Teleportation

Interpreting quantum teleportation could be difficult, as it exploits the feature of quantum mechanics that defies our classical way of thinking. Through our VR simulation, we aim to make this interpretation slightly less daunting.

With the square particle successfully teleported, it's vital to note that only information about the particle's state was transmitted. No physical entity traveled from one avatar to the other. Quantum teleportation here substantiates the potential for ultra-secure communication channels, as any attempt to intercept the communication would disrupt the quantum states and reveal the intrusion.

8.4. Quantum Entanglement, Teleportation, and VR

Understanding quantum entanglement and teleportation's convoluted concepts remains a significant challenge. The mystical realm of quantum physics pushes the boundaries of reality as we know it. Thanks to pioneering initiatives of virtual reality, these phenomena can be explored and understood in a novel, three-dimensional perspective.

As indicated by our VR experience, while we're far from teleporting humans or objects, we're making significant strides in transmitting quantum information. This lays the groundwork for future quantum networks, revolutionising communication, computation, and cybersecurity.

In conclusion, let this VR journey through quantum entanglement and teleportation serve as a reminder that the universe holds unfathomable mysteries and immense potential. Despite quantum physics' complexity, its exploration in an interactive, immersive VR context makes the abstract tangible, underlining the quintessential role of emerging technology in deciphering the universe's profound enigmas.

It's not a journey that ends here; it's merely one speck of the incalculable cosmos. As you continue to navigate the universe's quantum mechanics corners, remember each concept, like the entangled particles, is interconnected, forming a nuanced, intricate web that is the fabric of reality itself. The navigator makes the journey as enlightening as the destination - in the case of quantum physics, every learning engaged in the VR experience is a revelation in itself. Welcome to the quantum adventure.

Chapter 9. Exploring Quantum Gravity: Bridging VR and the Edge of Physics

In the realm of Quantum Physics, one concept that continues to elude even the brightest minds is that of Quantum Gravity. Here, we begin to tread the often harrowing path of extending our understanding, aided by the transformative field of Virtual Reality.

9.1. The Hazy Intersection of Quantum Mechanics and General Relativity

The integration of Quantum Mechanics, which accounts for the smallest particles and their interactions, and General Relativity, the beautifully eloquent theory of gravity introduced by Einstein, has been one of science's most profound challenges. We see the solidity of General Relativity when we observe large scale cosmic phenomena, such as black holes or the overall expansion of the universe. Yet, when we scrutinize the smallest subatomic particles, Quantum Mechanics reveals itself in all its probabilistic glory.

However, when these two theories approach each other–at the extreme conditions of black holes or the big bang–they collapse into a profusion of infinities, rendering them useless. This hints at an incompleteness in both theories. Enter Quantum Gravity – a still nascent and theoretical field aiming to serve as the bridge between Quantum Mechanics and General Relativity.

9.2. Quantum Gravity: The Core Conundrum

In providing a consistent quantum description of gravity, one is attempting to combine the basic principles of quantum mechanics with the geometric nature of gravity. Quantum Gravity serves to eliminate the anomalies present when quantum field theories are applied to a curved space–time. However, our best efforts to materialize a workable theory have yet to completely succeed.

The primary obstacle arises from our current understanding of quantum mechanics, which describes nature as fundamentally stochastic, while general relativity is inherently deterministic. This discrepancy prompts the need for a new paradigm in our exploration of the universe, one that reconciles these jarring discrepancies.

9.3. The Virtual Reality Conduit

The transformational capabilities of Virtual Reality (VR) come into play precisely at this crossroads. VR serves as a powerful tool to mentally model and intuitively grasp the amorphous shape of Quantum Gravity, blurring the lines between the perceivable reality of our daily life and the conceivably unmanifested potential of the quantum realm.

Using VR's immersive and interactive capabilities, we can create a dynamic model of Quantum Gravity. This simulated spatial environment gives us the 'feel' of the universe on quantum scales, enabling us to more naturally understand the currently abstract theories.

9.4. Map of the Quantum Realm: No Prior Scale

The first step of the process requires constructing a 'map' of the Quantum Realm. It's important to consider that in the Quantum Realm, there is no prior geometry or spatial structure, a radical departure from our macroscopic reality. This has several paradoxical implications that become challenging to grasp. VR's ability to create simulations can allow us to navigate this unusual realm, granting us a visceral understanding of this profoundly distinct space-time.

9.5. Uncertainty Embodied

Another concept central to quantum physics is Heisenberg's Uncertainty Principle – aiming to reflect this in our virtual realm brings about its own hurdles. Allowing users to 'feel' the inherent uncertainty and display the probabilistic nature of particles with varying degrees of certainty, akin to 'clouds', helps grasp their inherent 'unsettled' existence.

9.6. Strategizing The Quantum Jumps

A further significant challenge lies in comprehending quantum superposition and quantum collapse. In our quantum VR, initially all particles can exist in superposition states. Observing a particle would trigger the quantum collapse, forcing it into one state, emulating the infamous Schrodinger's Cat Paradox.

9.7. The Dance of Entangled Particles

Fascinating quantum phenomena like entanglement can also be showcased in a VR environment. Entangled particles, no matter their astronomical separation, would instantly respond to changes in one another's states - an elegant ballet of intertwined existence.

9.8. Visualizing Gravity as Curvature

The geometric gravity of Einstein can be visualized as curvatures within our VR model. Given that there are no forces in General Relativity, but only the curvature of space-time, in our imaginary world, planets and stars would curve the space around them, exhibiting the force we perceive as gravity.

9.9. Quantum Gravity: A VR Perspective

The culmination of incorporating these individual elements create an embryonic understanding of Quantum Gravity. In the virtual world, Gravity would no longer be a force transmitted by particles, but something more profound and inherently tied to the fabric of space-time.

9.10. Quantum Leap Forward

By leveraging VR's capabilities to this fantastical realm, we might open possibilities to make huge advancements – not just by its visually enticing impressions, but more importantly, for its capability to impart an intuitive understanding of the elusive Quantum Gravity.

This might well serve as the foundation for the break-through realization required to finally unearth a robust theory.

The realm of Quantum Gravity, distinct, disarming, and yet, enchanting, has been, for the first time, laid out in our VR model, a testament to our pursuit of deciphering nature's most cryptic codes.

Chapter 10. Beyond Ordinary: Quantum Field Theory in Virtual Reality

Understanding the Quantum Field Theory (QFT) is less about delving into the arcane and more about stretching the boundaries of our perceptive capacities presented by our senses. It is a world where particles are born from vacuum, annihilating each other to create nothing, a bewildering place where principles of cause and effect can temporarily seem to all but disappear. Yet, our reality is securely grounded in the foundations set by quantum field theories; they form the architecture of the Universe at its most fundamental relationship of mass and energy. Let's embark on this exciting journey of understanding QFT through the immersive possibilities offered by Virtual Reality (VR).

10.1. Vacuums, Fields and Particles

In the quantum world, a vacuum is far from being empty. Here, spontaneous creation and annihilation of particle-antiparticle pairs occur sporadically, thus forming the incredibly dynamic quantum vacuum. This might appear a violation of the energy conservation principle until you get introduced to the concept of fields underlying everything in the cosmos.

Fields, as per QFT, are not just mathematical constructs, but the actual reality; infinitely extended objects that permeate the entire universe. Each type of particle corresponds to a unique quantum field. Photons for the electromagnetic field, electrons for the electron field, and so forth. When a particular field goes under a transition from a higher energy state to a lower one, we perceive it as the creation of a particle in the field. Enter this through VR, and you're in for a roller coaster ride of visually experiencing the birth and death of particles happening ceaselessly.

10.2. Entanglement: The Quantum Quandary

The quantum world keeps its fascination up with the intriguing phenomenon of entanglement, where particles are interconnected irrespective of the distance between them. Change the quantum state of a particle, and its entangled partner's state will alter instantly, even if it's light-years away. This "spooky action at a distance", as named by Einstein, challenges our most deep-seated perceptions of reality.

Visualising entanglement in VR breaks these barriers. Imagine two entangled electrons, visualized in VR as spheres, spinning in opposite directions. Alter one's state, and the partner reacts simultaneously, effectively conveying the baffling quantum correlation. The VR rendering of entanglement beautifully captures this non-local phenomenon, thus bringing within grasp the clash between quantum mechanics and relativity.

10.3. The Quantum Realm: A Dance of Fields

While visualizing the particle-based picture given by quantum mechanics had its limits, QFT beckons a shift of perspective – the particle-wave duality. Particles in QFT are pictured as excitations or vibrations of the quantum fields, akin to how waves are in an ocean. Thus, the whole cosmos is a gigantic orchestration of these vibrating fields, each field playing its part, resulting in this intricate and complex universe.

Experiencing this with VR gives us an artistic narrative, where we can wander in a visual symphony of interconnecting fields resulting in a mesmerizing 'dance of fields'. It is a direct plunge into the undulating world of the quantum, where one observes the harmoniously chaotic nature of the cosmos, unlike anything else.

10.4. Interacting Fields: Birth of Virtual Particles

Interactions between fields form the crux of QFT. Think of a photon energy packet travelling in an electromagnetic field, hitting an electron, and causing it to move. This intimate interaction, visualized in VR, portrays a magnificent ballet of fields crossing paths and creating dazzling, temporary particles, intriguingly described as virtual particles.

Virtual particles aren't particles per se, rather disturbances caused by field interactions, fundamentally shaking the mechanics of the quantum world. The activity of these virtual particles forms the basis for understanding the forces that drive the cosmos, such as the weak and strong nuclear forces, along with the electromagnetic force.

10.5. Reinventing Reality: Quantum Teleportation

Virtual reality transporting us into the heart of quantum mechanics paves the way for understanding quantum teleportation. Unlike science fiction, it does not involve moving objects physically. Instead, it's about teleporting the quantum state of a particle onto another, distant particle.

Teleportation, visualized through VR, walks us through a succession of quantum processes — entanglement, quantum state measurement, quantum transmission, and quantum jump. Straddling the fine line between the incredible and the impossible, this makes for an awe-inspiring VR journey, taking us a step closer to grasping the quantum mystique.

Pervading this journey, brought alive by VR, with the ineffable phenomena of the quantum world, the complexities of Quantum Field Theory transpose from mere abstractions to digestible, tangible experiences. As we move from traditional ways of understanding to experiential learning, unparalleled insights into the enthralling realm of QFT unfurl, surpassing boundaries of ordinary comprehension.

Chapter 11. The Quantum Future: Opportunities and Implications of VR in Quantum Physics

Diving headfirst into the intriguing world of quantum physics promises to be an enigmatic journey, one that is made infinitely more immersive and comprehensible through the might of virtual reality (VR).

11.1. Break Down of Quantum Realm

Quantum mechanics is a branch of physics that seeks to explain the quirky behavior of subatomic particles. These bewildering entities, which include electrons, protons, and neutrons, to name a few, are subject to a different set of rules than those dictating our macroscopic world.

You might wonder, for instance, why we can't teleport like an electron does, disappearing in one spot and, in the blink of an eye, reappearing elsewhere. This strange phenomena is an example of quantum superposition, a principle that states a quantum system can exist in multiple states simultaneously until it's observed. Another wonder of the quantum world is entanglement, where particles become inseparable twins, reflecting each other's states instantaneously irrespective of the physical distance. While these principles are shrewdly elusive, they aren't totally resistant to understanding. If demystified, these challenges could invite untapped opportunities.

11.2. VR as an Educational Tool in Quantum Mechanics

VR, with its capability of providing engaging and experiential learning, is an optimal tool for deconstructing the abstract principles of quantum mechanics. VR has proven effective across multidisciplinary research, where it can create transformative, interactive experiences. Digital renderings mimic the quantum world, rendering otherwise abstract concepts into a perceivable reality.

Applications like "Quantum VR" indeed take you on an exhilarating journey into the quantum realm, allowing individuals to interact with particles, observe their various states and understand the unique laws that govern them. VR effectively bridges the cognitive gap between the macroscopic world we live in and the microscopic world of quantum particles.

11.3. Implications and Opportunities for Scientific Research

With the advent of VR, researchers are no longer limited to simple 2D simulations. Full-scale quantum simulations are now possible, where scientists can interact with and observe phenomena otherwise impossible in the real world.

Imagine being able to 'watch' a wave function collapse, or create and destroy quantum particles at will. This immersive observation will divulge pivotal information about the quantum world, leading to expedited research progress in quantum computing, cryptography, and teleportation.

11.4. Quantum Teleportation and VR

Quantum teleportation, a process where the state of a particle is transferred from one place to another without any physical movement, can be understood much more effortlessly with VR. The process previously confined to complex mathematical equations can now be visually rendered and interacted with. It opens up a realm of possibilities for teleportation on a macro scale.

11.5. Quantum Computing and VR

In the field of quantum computing, VR can aid in the design and understanding of qubits, the fundamental unit of quantum information. Developing robust quantum computers is a colossal challenge due to the extreme sensitivity of particles. However, VR lets scientists actively engage with these particles in immersive simulations, potentially speeding up progress in quantum computers.

11.6. The Challenge of Presenting Quantum Physics through VR

One crucial point to acknowledge is the challenge of translating abstract ideas into Virtual Reality. It requires immense creativity, technological know-how, and a deep understanding of both disciplines. We are tasked with upholding scientific accuracy while translating these complex concepts into a visual, interactive medium.

Moreover, VR simulations, by their nature, are subject to our macroscopic laws of physics. Applying these when simulating the quantum world could create certain inaccuracies. However, this is a challenge to overcome, not a barrier that halts progress.

While hurdles undeniably exist, the intersection of VR and quantum physics holds remarkable promise. We stand on the brink of a new era where these two groundbreaking technologies will transform our understanding of the universe and forge a new path for scientific discovery.

In conclusion, VR's intersection with quantum physics offers radical possibilities for education, research, and understanding. It heralds a future where seemingly unfathomable principles of the quantum world are made visually and experientially accessible, further driving our collective curiosity and understanding of the universe. This quantum future, then, does not appear as a perplexing mystery but as an exhilarating voyage, waiting to be embarked upon. This interdisciplinary union of VR and quantum physics illuminates a path toward this quantum future - a future made conceivable through the immersive experience of Virtual Reality.

www.ingramcontent.com/pod-product-compliance
Lightning Source LLC
Chambersburg PA
CBHW071011260726
48661CB00007B/2888